BLOOM

A journey of love & healing

ANJALI MALIK

Cover design by Adarsh Thakkar
Illustrations by Anjali Malik

To the loving people in my life

CONTENTS

Paintings

We are all paintings
Unique in our own ways
With strokes of perfection
And stripes of imperfection

We are all paintings
Some look at us with exuberance
Others with skepticism
As if we are all not craze

We are all paintings
Unparalleled combinations and imitations
With our own limitations
Waiting to be understood

We are all paintings
Wanting to be seen
Longing to be found
Holding ourself with every thread
We are all just paintings

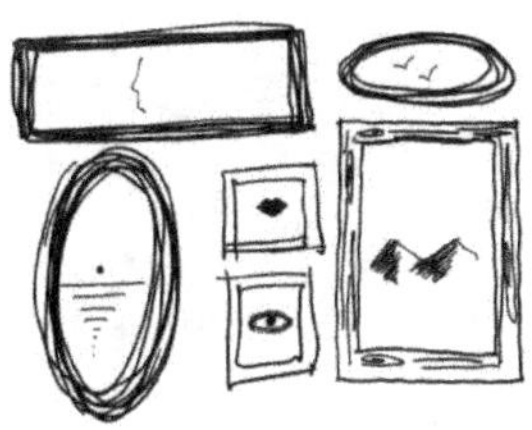

Wanted

If you ever feel small
Just remember

You exist
with aurora stars
waterfalls galaxies
sunflowers fireflies
rainbows forests

The universe wants you

Love

I thought I wanted someone
Who knew struggle like I do
But I want someone
Whose hands know the way to mine
Even before I extend mine

In love

Is the sea
In love with the sun?
Does he wait
For the evening to arrive
So the sun melts into his arms

Is the sky
In love with the birds?
That she watches from above
As they come
And gives them space to fly

Are the stars
In love with the night
That they light up with happiness
When the night arrives

Are the trees
In love with the rain
That they protect them from falling
As they trust them to hold them

Extraordinary

It takes courage
To write about your imperfections
Lovingly
To accept that you're only human

To see every detail
Every stretch mark
Every wrinkle on your body
And hug it 'cause it's you

To stay in your body
Not in your thoughts
Experience where it feels heavy
And let it go

To look at yourself
With curiosity
And compassion
Instead of judgment

To see yourself
As ordinary
Which is what makes you
Extraordinary

Kind embrace

Be kinder
Specially to the parts of you
which you feel are imperfect
broken or ugly

Be kinder to the parts
That you have tried to hide
And those
that you try so hard to avoid

'cause all of you
Deserves kindness and love

Beyond Labels

You are not
What others say you are
It's for you to decide
Don't let people
Put you into a box
And give you a label
You're beyond that
You're too amazing
to be defined by a word

A love like that

It's not the passionate
firework kind of love
that I seek
I look for the comfort
of being imperfect
And yet be looked at
with a loving gaze
I crave for the lack
of masks that we both
put on to be admired
I want to be wanted
for the way I am
and not just the way I look
I wait for the kind of love
where the comfort
isn't enslaved by words
I want the kind of love
that is shared by
sun and moon
Where the moon comes up
when the sun needs to rest
and sun pours its light
for the moon to shine

Self love

It's the time
when everyone talks about
Self love
But can flowers exist
in isolation?
Don't they need
soil
water
care
and loving hands
to bloom
Love is created
not in isolation
but
between people

Self doubt

What if clouds doubted themselves
Thought they were loud dark and big
What if they were unsure of their charm
What if they couldn't see
How they mesmerize us
with their existence
How everyone wants to capture the sky
'cause their mere presence
makes everything magical

Seek your forgiveness

Forgive yourself
For the mistakes you made
And the people you trusted
even though they didn't deserve it
Forgive yourself
For you didn't know better
but darling you did your best
with the knowledge you had
Your heart is pure
And you are courageous
That you put your trust
in their hand
It's not on you
that they were not worthy of it
It's not on you 'cause
you cannot know everything
So now that you know better
Forgive yourself
and let yourself be

Good riddance

No true relation breaks
When you speak your truth
Show them who you are
The sky doesn't get scared
When the clouds thunder
rather it makes place for them
to pour their heart out

Is life fair?

Do daisies ever feel
that life is unfair
Lotuses are looked at with awe
and roses are desired by all
Lilies are celebrated and adored

Do waterfalls ever feel
that life is unfair
Rivers get to travel
and streams do as they wish
Oceans have it all

Do mountains ever feel
that life is unfair
Waves caress the beach sand
and forests protect the land

Or do they see
Daisies get everyone to smile
Waterfalls can even mold the earth
And mountains are embraced by
the streams & cherished by the herbs

You are the ocean

You are not the pond
that everyone calls you
You are the ocean
capable of engulfing storms
and smothering fire
Carrying stories of resilience
yet wearing your calm
You are
the unfathomed deep ocean
that cannot be deciphered by all

Breaking Patterns

Today once again
My old pattern knocks at my door
Wearing a blanket of meteors
A sight not unfamiliar to me
He promises me Roses
but this time
I can also see the thorns
and refuse to dance along
I remember how alluring the roses are
But I know
Thorns always leave a scar

You deserve the full heart

You don't deserve
Halfhearted love
Or uncertainty
You deserve someone
Who loves you with their whole heart
Through actions and words
Someone who doesn't leave you confused
and wanting for more
You don't deserve those crumbs
They call love

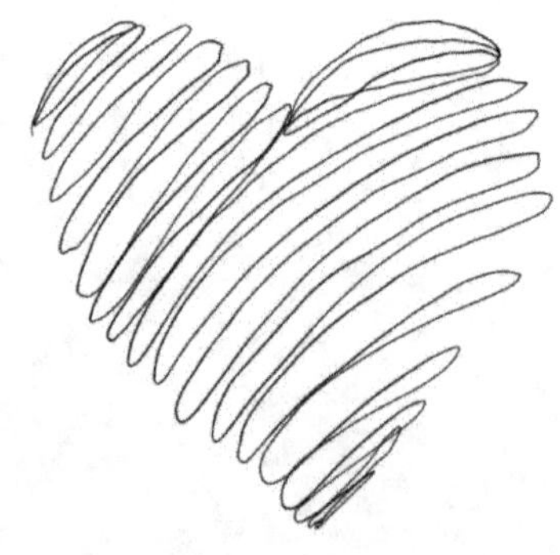

You're worth the universe

What you need
Matters
You don't have to be small
indirect or less
For your needs to be seen and met
You deserve to ask for what you need
You're not being too much
You're not being extra
You're just asking for what you want
And
You're worth every bit of the effort
You're worth the universe

Hope

I hope
In all the places you felt
Insecure
Small
Unworthy
You feel accepted, loved
and seen by yourself

I hope flowers bloom
and light enters
through crevices
which were once scars

And

I hope
You see the universe
inside you
Which makes your heart glow

Nebula

When everything seems
broken and you feel lost
Remember
Once in a while
when a star explodes
it gives birth to
a beautiful nebula
Where new stars
are born
You are not broken
or lost
You are transforming
leaving your old self
and creating your own nebula

Grades on your marksheet

People gave you a unit to measure your worth
The grades on your marksheet
The ranking of your college
The number on a weighing scale
The number of your followers
But
No number can define you
Or decide your value
You are worthy
and invaluable

Change

The anger of unwanted touch
The pain of broken trust
The hurt of monstrous words
Will slowly fade
With loving words
caring touch
and affectionate people
Like the trees grow new leaves
and the old ones leave
with the onset of spring

Judgement

Judgement is the easiest thing to make

Requires no thought or curiosity
Only a lack of empathy

Where is the freedom to be?
If all I'm trying is to please

What's the point of perfection?
If the process isn't seductive

How good is the need to be at the top?
If it's fueled by fear not love

What good is this judgment?
If it's taking you far from your own self

Waiting

There's a universe inside me
Waiting
To meet the universe
In you

Moon doesn't show up the same everyday

Some flowers don't bloom every day
Rainbows don't exist in their glory
all the time
And moon doesn't shine the brightest
on cloudy days
and yet they are magnificent
You my darling
don't have to be perfect
or show up the same every day
to be magnificent

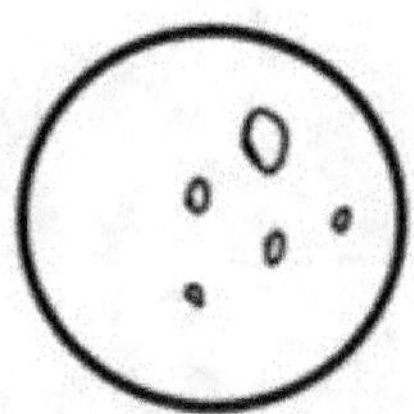

Dandelion

I was at a loss of words
bewildered
I stood there
You seemed like a dandelion
I wanted to save
I got up with the courage
to articulate comfort
Held you in an embrace
In that moment
I realized
You were not the dandelion

Emotions

Aren't emotions
ways we talk to ourselves?
Jealousy is you expecting more from yourself
Anxiety is care overpowering
and
Anger is a reminder of your boundaries

Moving on

No one teaches you
How to process death
How to move on from it
Should you stay strong
and not drop a tear
'cause you have to be there for everyone
Or let yourself and your body
feel the shock
let the grief in
take its time
and when you're ready
Let it go as well

Don't aspire to be liked

You were born in the hearts
of twinkling stars
With the wisdom of deep forest
Carrying the strength of mountains
and voice of thunder
Darling
You were not born
just
to be liked

Not in your hands

You can't control people
You can't stop them
from judging you
What you can control
is
doing what you want

Stars don't concern themselves
with the opinion of others
They just sparkle

Loving gaze

Reach out to that part
of you
that wants to fix others
love people out of their pain
That part of you
is deserving
of your loving gaze

River of love

When you left
I turned my tears
into poetry
And now it looks like
The love you left behind

Limitless

In this disposable world
Let me be a mountain
Persevering standing tall on his ground

In this mortal world
Let me be water
Changing shapes and color

In this rigid world
Let me be a climber
hugging the old buildings

In this unkind world
Let me be a tree
Ready to give what one needs

In this black and white world
Let me be a rainbow
Living without binaries

A *little less ugly*

When the mirror saw
details the camera couldn't capture
She thought it would yell out her flaws
To her surprise it was kinder
When the mirror spoke
it was like a gentle kiss on the cheek
and she felt a little less ugly

Good enough

You struggling to prove
You are good enough
To be chosen
But look who is choosing
Form shape color
Nothing matters
'cause it's not love darling
Its you running away
From your fears

Dare

I wish that you dare
To love yourself so much
That the opinions of others
Would seem like noise to you

I wish that you love yourself
With all you have got
With every cell of your body
And beats of your heart

I wish that you dare
To love yourself so much
That your eyes won't search for others
To tell you your worth

I wish that you love yourself
With words, thoughts and actions
Without asking for perfection
With no apprehension

I wish that you dare
To love yourself so much
That you don't turn towards anyone
For the love that is yours

Journey of self love

The warmth of a bare body
Hiding
A story inscribed all over it
Of the insecurities it inhabits

A body yearning for love
The touch of one's own tender heart
Searching for safety
Of an adoring hug

A body nurturing the hope
To be seen with all its invisible scars revealed
And be met with gentleness

A body caressing oneself
With words dripped in maple
And touch which feels like petals

The warm embrace of a bare body
Lying under the morning sun
Smiling and unabridged

Lovers

Everyone talks about
the sun and the stars
Forgetting the all expansive dark sky
in whose hands the Moon shines
Don't just be my Moon darling
be my sky!

Heart

You have a generous heart
That needs to be held
Gently
With love
Like a petal
holds the raindrop
in her lap

Desired

You were told
Roses are desired
They are what everyone wants
So even though
You were a sunflower
You tried to be
A rose
People called you alluring
they were enchanted
by your beauty
but the sunflower
remained alone
and unappreciated
As you failed to see it
You failed to see
it's beauty was unmatched
It was mesmerizing
like the twinkling of stars
was united with the halo of hope
and the happy colors of rising sun
were mixed in the ocean of love

Love doesn't care for perfection

Beyond the ideas of good and bad
Beyond the tall walls
which separate perfection from ordinary
Is your heart
Which doesn't care for it
All it craves is love

When the heart is promised
the love's embrace
If it crosses the wall
and reaches the field of perfection

The little heart drops everything
and runs in the pursuit of it
Turning a blind eye to the love
it wasn't promised but received
Forgetting what it really wanted

Neglect

I see the deserted house still standing
Enduring the pain of abandonment
Letting itself get engulfed by the creepers
Such is the pain of neglect
I wondered if I sat beside it
Resting my head on one of its walls
Will it cry?
Tell me the tales of those who inhabited it
or open his chest and let himself free

What hurts isn't love

Love doesn't bleed your hands
It caresses your soul
It's like stars coming together to make
constellations
Not galaxies existing years apart

Sharing

I thought there was power
In not sharing
In being strong taking it all with a smile
Not bothering those around you
Letting them believe
You have it easy
And that they can come to you
'cause you are strong
You don't have any worries
So you can listen and understand
Bake them a solution
Caress their wounds as you don't have any
I thought there was power
In not letting people see
that you are a human after all

Will you be loved?

You were standing at the crossroads
Making a deal with devil
It wasn't the best negotiation
You bargained authenticity
for a badge
of the good kid
Liked by everyone
Loved by all
You are still proud of it
even though it just sits
in the showcase of your house
that everyone admires
but you struggle to call home
The badge you hold so tight
You smile but your fingers bleed
from its sharp edges
The house that everyone loves
is not your home
You wonder if they see your home
With no showcase or badges
Will you still be good
Will you still be loved?

Be too much

For all the times
You have been told
You are too much
Darling
It's good to be too much
To care too much
To love too much
To give too much
There are people
Who are too less
Who are scared
of being too much
of giving too much
But you are not scared
So be too much!
Be the whole universe

Poems music and magic

There are poems
People don't want to read
Chords no one wants to hear
Nature's magic no one has seen
But they still are
poems music and magic

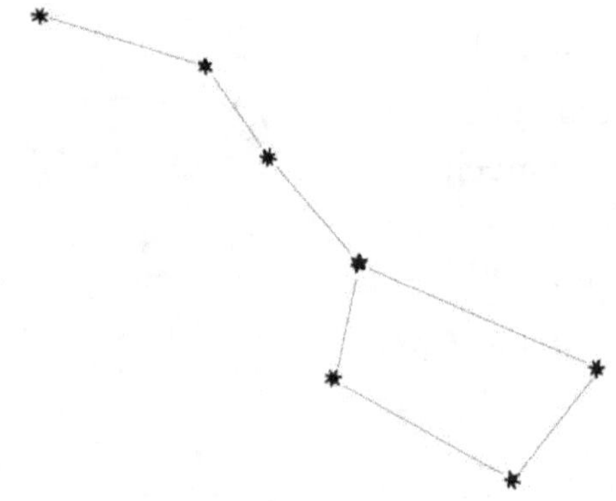

Love is in you

I saw the autumn tree
Brown
In his misery and pain
Of having lost
his beloved leaves
and wondered
If the longing
will ever end
It will
When he realizes
that the leaves
came from him

Significant

Born in neglected spaces
Do weeds wonder
Why they are not accepted
Do they want to belong
know that they are cared for
Do they fear being diminished
That they yearn to leave a mark on this world
Do they want to be significant
Make sure they are known
Are they scared of mountains
Who have outlasted everything on this earth
And want to make a place of their own
Do they wish to be known
Feel that they don't go unnoticed
Do weeds wonder
If they are loved

Let it go

Sometimes you have to make peace
with the incomplete
and stop fighting
Grieve the loss of a dream
the person who got away
the friendship you couldn't keep
the hope of a bond that you never got
your own past self
Grieve
Don't fight it anymore
And
When you are ready
Let it go

Can you trust

Can you trust
To let love in
with open arms
When it knocks at your door

Can you trust
That you won't be used
That people will keep their words
That you will find people
who will love you in many different ways

Can you trust
That you don't have to be perfect
for someone to see your worth
That you don't have to be someone else
in order to find love
That you don't have to do something
to deserve care

Can you trust
That things will fall into place
That you will meet the one
who is meant to be
That you can get without giving
That you are born for bigger things

Would you love me then?

I wondered
When you will see me up close
Raw
with just my bare self
Would you love me then?

When you will see
How my skin looks
With stretch marks and cellulite
Would you love me then?

When I'll turn on my bed
And the love handles
Won't look anything close to love
Would you love me then?

Will you be there
through my wrinkles and bad days
When I won't feel the best
Would you love me then?

Little did I know
The question wasn't for you
All along

Healing doesn't depend on apologies

Stop seeking an apology
from the same person
who has hurt you
Stop placing your healing
on another person
Forgive for yourself
Express for yourself
Let go for yourself

Pain

After years of stupor
The numbness was lost
An epiphany about the self
was all it took
for that anger to be felt
for everything to come back
Sitting down
Picturing pain
It felt like a teetotum
which moves but doesn't go away

Within you

Searching for love
You traversed thorny bushes
Climbed mountains of dead trees
Navigated deep oceans
Only to find that it was in you all along

Moon shines for you

You are not the moth
That dies waiting for the flame
to love her
you are the starry night
in love with moon
that shines for you

Things they didn't do

It's not just the things
people did that troubles
It's also the things
they didn't do

Neglect
Lack of curiosity
Making you feel unseen
Underappreciated
Are all things
someone didn't do

A lack of love isn't
just the wrong they did
but also
the right they didn't

Being you

There's a certain sense of peace
In not being famous
In not being extraordinary
As you are not living to excel or impress
You are not responsible for other people
There is no pressure which you bury yourself
under
You are just being yourself
Not caring if enough people like you
Or know you
You're the moon
Only caring about the next day
When the night arrives
and you just get to be you

You are magic

Too thin too fat
Too tall too short
Lies we tell ourselves
That
We have to fit in
The beauty standards
Which scream average
Look in the mirror
You buffoon
You are magic
You are a living breathing part
of this universe
You are here because
the universe saw you
as a perfect part of it

You are a flame

On the days
You find it difficult
to keep going

On the days
You search
for a purpose

Remind yourself
You are an ocean
with infinite depth
A flower
with power to bloom
The moon
with capacity to love
And a flame
with the fire of living

Giving up

Never give up
is overrated
I say
Give up
On things people patterns
that pull you down

Give up
On old ways
that no longer serve you
On self criticism
that doesn't help you
And validation seeking
that doesn't define you

Give up
On living with fear
and let go
On trying to fit in
and be your authentic self
On prioritizing everyone else
and choose you

Living in the moment

Flowers find their way to bloom at places they were
not even wanted.
Is it self-love?
Are they more aware and know their worth?
Have they dealt with the questions of existence?
Did they learn to live in the moment?
or
Do they bloom just because they can and know
their power?

Stardust

We are made of stardust darling
Embrace the galaxies of wisdom within you
And let it guide you
To the universe
Which is waiting for you

Heartbreak

At times
Heartbreak leaves you
With a gift
The gift of knowing

That your heart can be
As tender as a flower
And as strong as an armor

That it can shatter into
A thousand pieces like glass
And still form a kaleidoscope of colors
When it meets the sunlight

That it can turn into ashes
And yet rise again
'cause it is a phoenix

At times
Heartbreak leaves you
With a gift
The gift of knowing
Yourself

I thought it was love

I said I was attached
And thought it was love
Little did I know
It was fear speaking

I held on so tight
And thought it was love
Little did I know
Love didn't need to be held

I asked to stay
And thought it was love
Little did I know
Letting go was love too

I believed it was meant to be
And thought it was love
Little did I know
What is meant to be doesn't leave

Easy to love

You don't have to be perfect
You don't have to have no problems
You don't have to be too less
You don't have to be small
to make yourself easy to love

You don't have to fold yourself
to fit in a box others have designed for you
You don't have to mold yourself
to fit in other's expectations of you
You don't have to change
to make yourself easy to love

Be imperfect, be human
Have problems go out there
Be big
Dance outside the box
Spread your wings
Darling
You're not supposed to be easy to love!

Take space

You downplay yourself
Make yourself small
'cause it's hard to believe
But you are seen
Your struggle is seen
Take space
You are vast
Like the universe
Don't stop at the star

People are stories

People are stories
Stories are people

when you don't like
your story anymore

Remember you are the main character
And create a new one

Ask that voice

The voice in your head
Which calls you unworthy
Tells you that it's hard to love you
Which makes you question
anyone who chooses you
Which makes you fear
what would you be
If not those achievements
Which makes you scared
of disappointing those close to you

Ask that voice

How about you listen to yourself?
How about you tell yourself that
everyone would choose you without batting an eye?
What If you are worthy already?
What if other people's disappointment is not your
responsibility?
What if you are much more than your
achievements?
What is it that your heart desires?

You

I hope that you find someone
Who can love you out of your every insecurity
Your self doubts
Your fears
Your shame
I hope that you find someone
and
that someone is you

Belonging

You were made to feel like
you don't belong
Like you were different
You felt misunderstood
and scared the judgement
which labelled you a misfit
You felt isolated
in your experiences
but you're not alone

I see you
You belong right here
You were never born
to fit in
'cause you are far too beautiful
a soul
to be like everyone else

You're with me

Unfazed by the idea
of losing you
I walk ahead
As I have you with me
Woven in memories
Hidden in poems
It's like you stay
beneath my skin
In empty spaces
And the walls of my heart
'cause every beat
Is a reassurance
That you are
Indeed with me

Be soft

I don't wish you to be stronger
I know
That you are resilient

I wish you to be soft and let go of that strongness
sometimes
I wish you could melt and feel the warmth of love
like you deserve
I wish you see how love is waiting for you with
open heart
I wish you to trust others to be there and meet you
where you are
And believe that you don't have to be strong all the
time

On trusting

Before you trust
Before you pour your heart out
See if the vessel can receive it
If it has the strength to hold it
and not spill
The hammock is tied
not on a plant but a tree

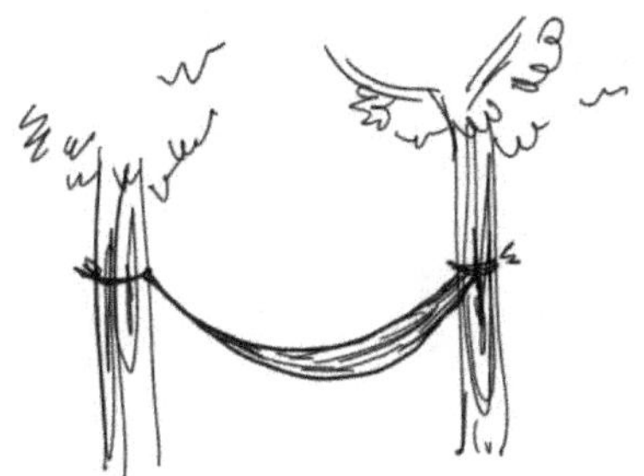

Love stayed

You made me
Fall in love with myself
and that love stayed
Even after you left

Flawless

I thought I was too courageous
Trying to find faults in me
Never looking away
from my flaws
But maybe
I shouldn't have focused
on my lacking

The earth isn't a perfect sphere
and the moon borrows its light
Yet they are flawless

The struggle wasn't mine

I could never reach you
It was like a void
between us
which love couldn't fill
I struggled
To reach your closed heart
To dismantle your guard
Break those walls
you have built around it

Then I realized
The struggle wasn't mine
to begin with

Happiness

Happiness is an emotion
Not a state
It seems unfair
to expect constant happiness
from life
And demand yourself to be happy
all the time

Would you appreciate rainbows
if they appeared everyday
Would you admire spring
if there were no fall and winter
Would you be enticed by happiness
if there were no other emotions to feel

You deserve the world

You deserve
To be seen & heard
To be held & loved
To be appreciated & validated
And all of it
without effort
My love
You deserve the world

Guilt of moving on

If you moved on
After losing a dear one
You have not forgotten them
Do not feel guilty
for living your life
Their love is with you

You living your life
is the evidence
of the love they left behind
When trees lose their flowers
they don't stop blooming
It is the love of those fallen flowers
that nourish the tree
to grow more flowers

Always

I was not a river
that would stay for a while
and let the bank go
I was the ocean
that fell in love
with the beach
and
kept coming back
to see him

Don't personalize everything

When you live near the equator
temperature in summers
can go up to 50 degrees Celsius

It's the same sun
we can't tolerate in summers
but love in winters

Don't personalize everything
you never know
where the person is coming from

Rise in love

It's so easy to fall in love with someone when you don't know them, they are an idea in your head, they can be anything and everything you want them to be. Only when you know someone you can't fall in love. You choose to love, you see the stretch marks, you see the scars, you see the enchanting eyes and innocent smile, you see the beauty and the imperfections. And then can choose to love, to rise in love.

On grieving

If you let grief
make its home
in your body
It becomes pain
Unless you hear it
Unless you understand it
Unless you give it
what it deserves
It won't leave

Sit with it
and when you feel ready
Let it go

And then
It will only remain
a visitor

Not your project

I wasn't looking to be fixed
Just
Loved

Your body deserves love for being

When I saw myself today
I didn't see stretch marks
or cellulite
What I did see
were the marks of being alive

My body carrying
her own unique prints
Singing that she feels alive

I didn't see the fat rolls anymore
There were no whispers
Only the voice calling them
a part of me
As there was a little more of me to love

There were no more questions
for you
'cause I have answered them
I don't have to wonder anymore
'cause I know
Love doesn't require eyes
but only sight

Voyage

If everything was fair
You wouldn't have gone through
the things you had to
If the world was a better place
You wouldn't have seen what
no child should see
But now you are an adult
You have power
You're amazing
strong
and resilient
You have faced things like a rock
And yet remained loving
That takes special courage
My darling
It's time that you realize
how far you have come
And be proud of the person
you have become

Have you seen love?

Has anyone kissed you twice cos they
missed it as soon as it ended?
Have you ever felt like thanking someone
for showing you how to love yourself
even when you don't look the best?
Seen someone make you smile when you are mad?
Make you flush just with their gaze?
Have you ever had someone trace every scar of
yours
with their magical fingers that left you at peace?
Were you ever overwhelmed by someone's selfless
kindness which can't be reciprocated?
Has anyone made you fall in love with yourself like
sky falls in love with the moon every night?
Has anyone held your heart where you were not
scared of clumsy hands?
Have you seen your insecurities disappear cos
you borrowed their eyes?
Have you
seen Love?

Your being deserves love

You're worth loving
You're worth all happiness in the world
Not because you are pretty
Or because of the things you do for others
But because you deserve it
Just
for being you

Intimacy

Hiding behind perfection
and decoding everything
Is your scared heart
Not shattered completely
but surrounded by huge walls

You are a rose
Tempting and alluring
But stings anyone
who tries to get too close
as your heart is yet to grieve
those promises people didn't keep
and accept love
It didn't feel it deserved

I want it to see
the magic that is universe
and find sunflowers
that dance to the tune of hope
'cause after the stormy night
the ocean too lets light through

Don't base your value on others

Don't let anyone's confusion
Decide your worth

There is strength in sharing too

You called me sensitive
'cause you were unaware
Running away from your emotions
To you it was a sign of weakness

There is strength
In bearing it all
without asking for a shoulder
But you never saw
there is strength
in sharing too

Even the clouds pour
when they are full

You are the Universe

Darling you are the universe
You are what makes the stars and breaks the rocks
Carries the sand dunes and occupies the moon
You make the snowflakes
And burn the forest
Shake the mountains
And form the rainbows
Darling you are the universe

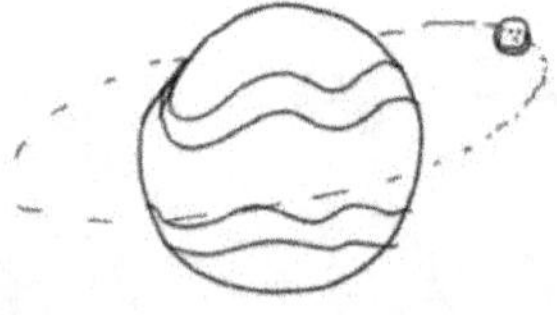

Love lives

We carry our loved ones
In the way we dress
and style our hair
In words they used
and tales they told
In ways we paint
and dance
In memories and in places
They stay with us
Cos love is created
Not in isolation
but between people
So they never leave
cos their love
Lives through us

Worth remembering

You do not exist to perform
or achieve
but experience
and enjoy
And while you are busy
doing what you love
you may
end up with something
worth remembering
and that's the beauty
of living

Move with love not guilt

You feel guilty
When you don't do the best

You feel guilty
When people are upset

You feel guilty
When everything you do isn't perfect

But
What if you did things
out of love and
not to escape guilt?

What if it was okay
To let people down
To do your best not the best
To just be you

I wish you knew love

I did not realise
you were never
looking for love

Just the assurance
that you were worth it

Darling just bloom

Lotus doesn't wait
for admirers
She doesn't look for others
to see her worth
She just blooms
As she knows
herself

Experiences don't define you

Your worth remains the same
Even if people leave

Voice of heart

Isn't poetry the voice of a broken heart
The laughter of an inner child
The desires of an artist working to make ends meet
Language of grief which never turned into tears
Closure for incomplete stories
Unsaid words of unrequited love
The Intimacy of lovers
Misplaced anger of unmet expectations
Solace in evenings of loneliness
The happiness of hearing a lover's voice
And the sadness of realization of our limited time!
Isn't poetry the voice of heart

Bloom

Bloom
Carefree
Like the sunflower outside your house
Proudly
Like the lotus in the pond
Happily
Like the marigold in your garden
Calmly
Like the parijat flower at night
Wildly
Like the purple weed on the streets
Childishly
Like the daisies on the field
Sensually
Like the rose in your backyard
Leisurely
Like the orchids in the shops
Bloom
You're not just a pretty flower

About the author

Anjali is a fresh and breathtaking voice in the world of poetry. She is a masterful wordsmith, with a distinctive and personal voice that is sure to leave a lasting impression. In Bloom, she explores themes of self-actualization that accompanies with falling in love and falling out of love. She gracefully takes the readers on a journey of self-discovery and contemplation. Inspired by the likes of Oliver and Gibran, Anjali intertwines her own experiences and those close to her to bring life to a myriad of emotions that almost all of us have experienced at some point in time.

Hailing from Rajasthan, and currently settled in Gujarat, the pandemic pushed her to reflect on the thoughts and feelings that have always been pushed away thanks to work and life. Once amorphous, those thoughts started taking shape as words on the paper and the feelings bloomed as aroma in the ink. A PhD scholar, a therapist, an amateur smiler, Anjali adds poet into her repertoire of skills with Bloom.

Instagram: @anjali_poetry_

www.ingramcontent.com/pod-product-compliance
Lightning Source LLC
LaVergne TN
LVHW041334200726
843509LV00009B/716